Finsbury Fields

The "Theatre"

The "Curtain"

Shoreditch

Spittle Fields

Moor Fields

Cripplegate

Moorgate

Bishopsgate

STREET

Houndsditch

Guildhall

Aldgate

CHEAPSIDE

The Mermaid Tavern

EAST CHEAP

GRACIOUS STREET

PENCHURCH ST

East Smithfield

Postern Gate

Green Hythe

TOWER STREET

St Saviour's

Bellings Gate

LONDON BRIDGE

THE TOWER

The "Globe"

SOUTHWARK HIGH STREET

Southwark

The distance from St Paul's to the Tower
is one mile: and from Bankside
to Shoreditch is one mile & a half.

# SHAKESPEARE AND THE PLAYERS

*A view of Shoreditch in* 1590, *showing the* Theatre *and the* Curtain *playhouses. In the distance is Old St Paul's.*

[*Frontispiece*

# SHAKESPEARE
## AND THE PLAYERS

*Written and illustrated by*
## C. WALTER HODGES, 1909–

*With a Foreword by*
## ALLARDYCE NICOLL

COWARD — McCANN, Inc.
NEW YORK CITY

1943

PRINTED IN GREAT BRITAIN

FOR
GRETA

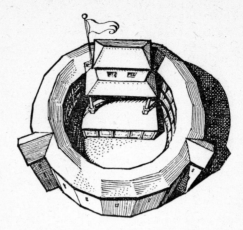

*. . . But pardon, gentles all,*
*The flat, unraised spirits that have dared*
*On this unworthy scaffold to bring forth*
*So great an object: can this cockpit hold*
*The vasty fields of France? Or may we cram*
*Within this wooden O the very casques*
*That did affright the air at Agincourt?*

From the Prologue to *Henry V.*

# Foreword

DESPITE ALL THE STUDY DEVOTED DURING the present century to the exploration of Shakespeare's stage, there is much that we do not know concerning both the structure of the Elizabethan playhouse and the methods employed by the actors in presenting their tragedies, histories and comedies to the public. At first glance it might seem as though we can never know more: unless a rare and happy chance unexpectedly turns up some new documents from some obscure corner, it is unlikely that any fresh evidence will come our way, and the documents already unearthed and published have frequently been analysed, compared with one another and related to such evidence as the plays themselves have to give to us.

The assumption, however, that we know all that can be known is erroneous; there is still room for further examination of this subject. In particular, we need to devote more attention than has been devoted in the past to individual theatres, with the object of determining how far the early London playhouses known as the Theatre, the Globe, the Swan and the Curtain exhibited common features and how far they differed from each other. Hitherto, only tentative essays have been made in this direction.

At the same time the general features of the Elizabethan public playhouse—the playhouse for which Shakespeare wrote and in which he spent his active years—require more closely to be related to contemporary Continental theatres. When we speak of the "Elizabethan stage" we are sometimes apt to let visions of half-timbered farmhouses delude our vision, and to forget both that the Renaissance styles in architecture were imposing themselves upon public buildings during those years when Shakespeare's fellows were building their stages and that the Elizabethan playhouse was part of a widespread theatrical development in Italy, France, Spain and the Netherlands. There is little justification for treating the English theatres in isolation or for crediting them with a primitive architectural form.

Mr. Hodges has taken these Continental models into consideration in his reconstruction of the Globe. There can be no question of "endorsing" any particular reconstruction made by a modern artist, since so many details can never be determined exactly and so many aspects of the Elizabethan theatre remain to be more fully discussed: but the opinion may be hazarded that, in the main, Mr. Hodges has here taken the right line. Even if we might challenge the exact placing of doors or pillars or windows, perhaps he has succeeded in giving us a general picture of the kind of thing contemporaries saw, and expected to see, when they had paid their pennies to the doorkeepers and stood, or sat, eager to listen to Marlowe's rich lyricism or to Shakespeare's finer harmonies.

It gives me very special pleasure to have the privilege of writing this foreword in view of the fact that Mr. Hodges' reconstruction is greatly influenced by the conclusions reached in a recent volume, *From Art to Theatre*, by my friend Professor George Kernodle. Professor Kernodle's examination of the interlocking Continental traditions in the theatrical world of the sixteenth and seventeenth centuries helps to provide the justification for Mr. Hodges' vision of the playhouse that first welcomed *Hamlet* and *Twelfth Night*, perhaps the most fortunate theatre in the entire history of stage endeavour and certainly among those best fitted to call into being the richest qualities of dramatic utterance.

ALLARDYCE NICOLL.

*July*, 1948.

9

# Acknowledgments

CHIEF AMONG THE BOOKS I HAVE USED IN MAKING the reconstruction of the Globe Playhouse shown on pp. 62 and 63 are *The Globe Playhouse: Its Design and Equipment* by John Cranford Adams; *From Art to Theatre* by George R. Kernodle; and *The Elizabethan Stage* by Sir Edmund K. Chambers. I would also like to take this opportunity of thanking Mr Walter H. Godfrey, F.R.I.B.A., whose own reconstructions of Elizabethan playhouses are so well known, for much helpful criticism and advice. It is proper to add, however, that my reconstruction differs in one respect or another from the various solutions given by these authorities.

The colour plate used as a frontispiece to this book, and the headpiece to Chapter 1, together with some of the matter in Chapter 3, were first published in *Junior*, and are reprinted here by kind permission of Children's Digest Publications Ltd.

C.W.H.

# Contents

# Illustrations

## 1. *The Strolling Players*

WHEN WILLIAM SHAKESPEARE WAS A BOY there was no such thing in all England as a theatre. Nobody had ever heard of a building specially kept for the performance of plays. Play-acting, the little there was of it, had always been done on wooden scaffolds in market-places, streets and yards, as part of the celebration of the great festivals of the Christian year. The plays, usually derived from stories in the Old Testament, were acted by the townsfolk themselves. Each of the guilds of a town would have its own scene, and its own little stage: the Skinners' Guild would do the story of Noah, the Grocers' the Judgement of Solomon, the Butchers' Daniel in the Lions' Den, and so on. But this kind of play-acting was very old even when Shakespeare was young, and was slowly being forgotten. Instead, the townsfolk of the provincial towns of England, even of small towns like Stratford-on-Avon (where Shakespeare was born in 1564), looked forward to the summer visits of the players from London.

These were professional actors who had formed themselves into companies, each under the patronage of some nobleman whose livery they were entitled to wear; thus one company would call itself the Earl of Sussex's Men, another Lord Hunsdon's Men, and so on. There was even a company of Queen Elizabeth's Men. Their titles were very high-sounding, but I doubt that to meet a company of players going along the road on a dusty afternoon between one town and the next, you would have thought them much to look at. There would be about nine or ten of them, with a couple of lads who played women's parts (since it was thought disgraceful for real women to appear on the stage) and they travelled, some on foot, some on horseback, carrying all their gear in baskets on a donkey. They had playbills printed stating who they were and what they were going to act, and one or two of them would go ahead to paste them up, and make all the arrangements at the next town. They went first to the mayor, and if he thought well of them he would invite them to play at the town hall, and he himself would honour them by being present at their first performance. But at other places, or if there was no suitable hall, they might have to put up their stage in the yard of the inn.

Players were not always welcome among the more respectable people. "Hark, hark, the dogs do bark, the beggars are coming to town: Some in rags and some in tags and some in scarlet gown." Say "players" instead of "beggars" and you have a good idea of how they appeared to many self-respecting people of Shakespeare's day. At least, of his early days.

Their performances were of all kinds: plays, clowning, dancing, juggling, or acrobatic shows; they had to be ready for anything. Their standard of performance was high, and many of their companies were famous not only throughout England, but in places overseas. In Holland, Germany and Denmark there are many old record-books which tell of visits by "The English Comedians".

We know from the records at Stratford that the players were often there. Probably they came regularly once a year. Shakespeare, so far as we know, lived all his boyhood there. His father was a well-to-do tradesman, one of the aldermen of the town, and William went to the Stratford Grammar School. He must often have stopped to watch the players coming down the street, all in their motley clothes, with drum and trumpet before them, like any circus parade in a country town nowadays; and if so we may be sure he would follow behind them with the other boys, and push his way into the Guildhall to see the show.

## 2.  *The Queen at Kenilworth*

When Shakespeare was eleven years old Queen Elizabeth came in state to Kenilworth, where she stayed for three weeks at the castle as guest of the great Earl of Leicester. All her courtiers came with her, with all their servants and men-at-arms. The occasion, known since then as the Princely Pleasures of Kenilworth, is remembered as having been the most splendid display of pageantry in her reign—a reign famous for pageantry. Day after day there were hunting and feasting, plays and masques and dances, the shooting off of cannon by day and fireworks by

night, with everywhere music and fine dresses.
Kenilworth is only a walking distance from
Stratford and it would be very surprising if young
Will Shakespeare did not go there with his family,
among the crowds from all the near-by places, to
see something of the spectacle; and perhaps he
may have had a glimpse of some of the theatrical
displays which were given in the Queen's honour
on the lawns before the castle.

Such displays, though they were not often on so
large a scale, were not uncommon; indeed Queen
Elizabeth, like all great sovereigns of her time,
whenever she travelled in state through the
country, would expect to be received with cere-
monial pageantry at every important town she
came to. Much money and skill were spent upon
the presentation of these shows, which usually
took the form of recitals of music and poetry
given by people dressed as characters of British or
classical mythology, such as Hercules or Queen
Mab; or somebody dressed as the founder or
patron saint of the town would come to welcome
the Queen within the gates. All this would be
done with lavish decoration on ornamental
stages, or with triumphal arches surmounted by
figures in pageant dress, scattering flowers and
perfumes on the Queen as she passed by. Or the
show might be given on the waters of a lake. This

was a favourite device. At Kenilworth there was
a water display in which the Lady of the Lake
was carried off by Orion riding on a dolphin. At
another entertainment given for the Queen by the
Earl of Hertford some years later, the Earl had
had prepared a whole artificial lake, complete
with three "islands" in it. One was built up to
represent a ship, full of cannon to fire salutes for
the Queen; one a fort; and one a hill shaped
rather like a snail shell, and so called a "Snail

Mount". Upon the lake there floated a little pinnace, with a nymph and her maidens in it singing, and this was pulled along to the shore, where the Queen awaited it, by a group of people representing Neptune and his attendant Tritons, dressed "with grisly heads and beards of divers colours and fashions". This is the scene which I show in the picture above.

The actors in these performances were usually ladies and gentlemen of the Court; but professional players were often employed as well, probably for the longer speaking parts where trained voices were required. The Earl of Leicester had his own company of players, which would certainly have been at Kenilworth during the Queen's visit. This company was led by a certain James Burbage, who may rightly be said to be one of the founders of the English theatre as we know it to-day, because on his return to London after the Pleasures of Kenilworth, in the year 1575, he opened the first public theatre ever built in England.

### 3.   *The First "Plaie Howses"*

In the autumn most of the players' companies returned from the country to winter quarters in London, where they performed throughout the winter. Before James Burbage built his theatre the best places for these performances, in London as in the country, had been the open yards of the great inns. If you will look at the map of old London in this book you will see Gracious Street (it is called Gracechurch Street to-day), which was a part of the great main road going north and south through the City. It was here, and along the main streets crossing it, that the principal inns were found, and here, when the plays were on, all the street outside would be crowded with folk going in. They were not always the best kind of people either. All the commotion, the blocking of the streets and the quarrelling, to say nothing of the hucksters and beggars it brought together, were naturally looked on with great dislike by the City authorities and the more respectable folk; and, as the plays were so often given on Sundays and on religious feast-days, they were especially disliked by those religiously minded people who were then beginning to be known as Puritans. Plays, said the Puritans, were "the nest of the Divel and the sink of all sin. . . . They are public enemies to virtue and religion; . . . and bring both the Gospel into slander; the Sabbath into contempt; men's souls into danger; and finally the whole Common-weal into disorder". The Lord Mayor wrote to the Privy Council complaining that the plays caused "unthrifty waste of money by poor persons, sundry robberies by picking and cutting of purses, uttering of seditious matters, and many other corruptions of youth, and other enormities; besides also sundry slaughters and maimings of the Queen's subjects, that have happened by falling scaffolds, frames, and stages, and by engines, weapons and powder used in plays". But for all these complaints, and many others like them, that were uttered from almost every pulpit in London, year in year out, the plays became increasingly popular, and larger and larger crowds gathered to see them. New plays, new poets, new actors had to be found to cope with the growing demand for this new field of entertainment which was rising almost out of nothing, just as in recent times the Cinema has grown up and become a part of everybody's life.

However, whatever else you may have thought about the rights and wrongs of going to the play in those days, there was one good reason for staying away which nobody could deny. Queen Elizabeth's London was never quite free of the plague. It came nearly every summer, and of course where there were big sweating crowds of people who didn't wash very often—and that, quite plainly, is what most of the people were like —the infection spread rapidly among them. In those days nobody knew what caused the disease; but since it so often seemed to start among the crowds at the play, respectable people used to think it came as a judgement from God upon the sinful places where play performances were held. In any event it was wisely decreed by the City Council that whenever the plague appeared in London all performances of plays should cease,

and when this happened the players packed up
and took themselves off into the country again.

The Lord Mayor and his Council tried hard
to get rid of the players altogether, but as all the
principal players' companies had powerful friends
and patrons at Court they never succeeded in
doing so. Doing what they could, however, they
at last managed to hedge the players around with
so many local regulations and restrictions, and
generally made life so difficult for them in the
City, that in the end most of the companies
found it more worth while to stay in the suburbs,
where the City Council had less control. This was
the situation when James Burbage returned from
Kenilworth, and he decided that although it was
a bad thing to be away from the easy crowds in
the centre of town, he might none the less turn
the situation to advantage. Away from the narrow
streets he would have room to build a "plaie
howse" of his own, capable not only of showing
his plays at their best, but also of holding much
larger audiences than could be crowded into an
inn. He borrowed some money and rented a
piece of ground in Shoreditch, which in those
days was at the end of a grassy little country
road—to-day's Bishopsgate Street—where people
used to go on holiday afternoons to watch the
archery practice in Finsbury Fields or the Tower

gunners firing off cannon in a place called the Artillery Garden. He rented his bit of ground for twenty-one years only. We shall have reason to remember that in a later page.

He built his "plaie howse" of timber. It had three open galleries, one above the other, surrounding a circular yard or arena,—an idea Burbage probably copied from the bear-baiting arenas on Bankside, the district on the south bank of the Thames. (Perhaps he reckoned that if the craze for plays fell off he could still use his arena for bear-baiting and suchlike things, instead.) Built out from one side of the yard into the middle was the stage, just a high bare platform. The surrounding galleries were roofed with thatch, but the arena, and probably the stage also, at least in the beginning, was open to the sky. Burbage called this experimental playhouse of his "The Theatre" (being short for "Amphitheatre"). He opened it in 1576.

His venture was such an immediate success that it must have surprised even Burbage himself, and in the following year he built another playhouse, right next door. This, too, prospered. It was called "The Curtain", because it was built on a piece of land called Curtain Field; and there is a street called Curtain Road over the site of it to this day. Shortly afterwards a rival company, run by a certain Philip Henslowe, opened a third playhouse, called "The Rose", over on Bankside.

These were the principal theatres that Shakespeare knew when he first came to London.

## 4. *Shakespeare comes to London*

Nobody knows for certain when Shakespeare first came to London, though it is generally believed it was in the late fifteen-eighties; perhaps in the year of the Armada, when he was twenty-four. Neither do we know why he left Stratford. There are a number of stories, among which is a favourite one telling how Shakespeare, an unruly young man, was caught poaching deer in Charlecote Park, the home of the local squire Sir Thomas Lucy, and that he fled from Stratford to escape the consequences. Something of the kind may have happened, and it may have led him, as some people think, to join a troupe of players who were passing through Stratford, and go with them overseas to the Low Countries: some say he even went as far as Italy. It is not at all unlikely, and there is much in his writing which seems to show he was very familiar with foreign travel. But the

28

most famous story of all is that, arriving in London poor and unknown, he took a job as a horse-boy outside the Theatre, minding the horses of well-to-do patrons while they were in at the play; and that he proved himself so ready and reliable at this job that people soon did not care to entrust their horses to anyone else, and Shakespeare had to employ a number of boys to help him, who used to run up to patrons as they arrived, calling "I am Shakespeare's boy, sir". Whether this is true or not, it is probable that Shakespeare started his theatrical life in a very modest way, sometimes acting, sometimes giving a helping hand backstage and copying out parts for the other players. And it is likely that he spent some time adapting and rewriting other people's old plays, before his own original genius began to be recognised. It should not be forgotten that although Shakespeare is the supreme poet of the English language he himself never lost sight of the fact that he was an actor writing for actors. He lived all his working life in the theatre as actor, writer and part-owner, and what he didn't know about the theatre, as a workaday job, wasn't worth knowing. But his theatre was so different from the sort of theatre with which we are familiar to-day that we shall do well to pause here, to look inside and see what sort of a place it was.

## 5. *A Day at the Playhouse*

In Queen Elizabeth's time the day started early. People were up and about by four o'clock: children were at school by six.

In the Theatre at Shoreditch, just when the early grey light was beginning, you might have heard a yawn from the place at the back where the actors dressed, and seen a man come sleepily out on to the stage to look at the new day. It was drizzling; there were puddles in the yard. The man looked up at the flagstaff which stood over the top of the house. Here every morning when the weather was fine he hoisted the house flag, which was the sign that a performance would take place that afternoon as usual, beginning at two o'clock. To-day he wouldn't hoist the flag just yet.

The man was one of the playhouse servants. He did duty as caretaker, stage-hand, and bill-poster, took walking-on parts in the afternoons, and did odd jobs generally. He went now and unbolted one of the doors in the yard and, seeing two or three of his friends already coming up the path to work, went out to the ale-house next door to get some beer for his breakfast.

When he came back it was broad daylight,

though still drizzly and grey. The stage-keeper had arrived, an oldish man who had been all his life with the players, and was now responsible for everything that went on backstage, just as a stage-manager is to-day. The man asked him, should he hoist the flag? The stage-keeper scratched his chin. Not yet, he said, leave it a little till Master Burbage came. He would be here shortly for this morning's rehearsal. Meanwhile take a broom and get on with sweeping out the top gallery.

James Burbage, who lived near by, arrived early at the Theatre with his son Richard (who in a few years' time was to become one of the two most famous players of his generation); and soon the whole company was with them, ready to start the day's work. The slow rain showed no sign of stopping. On any ordinary day, unless the rain were very bad, they would hoist the flag and risk it, but to-day was to be a special day, the first performance of a new play, when, according to custom, all entrance money would be doubled. Would people come in this weather? Would it not be better to wait till to-morrow? Meanwhile the author had arrived, and tethered his horse to a railing in the yard. He had just ridden out from the City hoping for the best, and now he stood with the others looking up into the wet sky. He thought he could see a bit of blue.

The author I have in mind for this one day at the Theatre is Thomas Kyd, and his play was *The Spanish Tragedy*, which was first performed in 1589. It became so popular that it ran, on and off, for fifty years. (Plays were not then performed for more than a few days at a time, but successful ones were repeated at intervals.) *The Spanish Tragedy*, a dark and baleful play full of ghosts, murders and revenges, was one of the great stage successes when Shakespeare first came to town, and he wrote his own *Titus Andronicus* in imitation of its bloodthirsty manner. That, too, was a success. But for the day that we are imagining Shakespeare was not yet on the scene, except as a small-part actor at the morning's rehearsal.

As the morning went on the sky began to brighten. The puddles in the yard began to shine, and only occasional drops of rain fell into them. Without waiting to be told, somebody went and hoisted the flag. Others went off to paste up play-bills in Gracious Street and Cheapside, by the main conduits where people drew water, and on the pillars in Paul's Walk, the nave of the Cathedral, which in those days was often more like a market-place than a church, and was where gentlemen of leisure went to walk and talk and show off their best clothes before dinner.

Dinner was at twelve o'clock. The gentlemen

in the town went to their eating-houses and talked about the afternoon's new play. At the Theatre the rehearsal was over, and the stage was being strewn with fresh rushes. Outside the entrance the side-shows were being set up: skittle alleys and tobacco booths, jugglers, quack doctors, fortune-tellers, apple-women, horse-boys, and a whole menagerie of rogues and beggars (such as Dommerers, who pretended to be dumb: Abraham-men, who pretended to be mad—"you see pinnes stuck in sundry places of their naked flesh, especially in their armes, only to make you beleeve they are out of their wits": and Priggers of Prancers—"To *Prig* signifies in their language to steale, and *Prancer* signifies a horse." They have been described for us in much detail by writers of the time).

The day had turned out fine after all, and there was a big crowd by the time the door was opened. Each person passing through put his coin into the box held there by a "gatherer". This first payment allowed him only to go in and stand in the yard among the "groundlings", but once there he could if he chose pay more money at a further entrance which led up from the yard to the galleries, and for seats in the best parts of the galleries there were further payments still. "A penny" is mentioned as the normal unit of payment, but it is difficult to estimate what this would mean in present-day values — probably something more in the region of a shilling. The most expensive parts of the house were the "Lords' Rooms" and "Gentlemen's Rooms", which were next to the stage, rather like the boxes in a modern theatre. As time went on, and more and more fashionable people began to go to the plays, there was not enough room in the boxes to take them all, and gentlemen began to sit out on the stage in front of them, on stools; and this custom eventually became so popular with the gallants and dandies, and at times there was such a crowd of them smoking and playing cards among themselves in everybody's view whenever they lost interest in the play, or loudly criticising the actors whenever they felt inclined, that in the end they became a thorough nuisance.

But on the day of this first performance of *The Spanish Tragedy* things had not got to that pitch. There would be nobody sitting on the stage. A few fine gentlemen, well-known patrons of the Theatre, were behind the stage watching the players getting into their costumes, or talking with the author and Master Burbage. The Lords' Rooms were already taken up. The better galleries were full and the rest were filling. Sellers of nuts and apples were doing a good trade, and

the boys from the ale-house were going in and out
with trays of pot ale. Somewhere there might be
a cutpurse waiting his chance; somewhere else
there might be a couple of quiet men whom
Master Henslowe, of the rival company at the
Rose, had sent along to write down as much of
the play as they could get, in shorthand. They
would come several times till they had it all pat,
and then Master Henslowe would be able to put
on his own pirated version of the play. All player
companies had to guard their plays jealously and
keep an eye open for this sort of thing, which was
not uncommon.

A trumpet now sounded from the top of the
house. It was the first of three soundings, and
warned the late-comers in the road to hurry; the
second sounding was a signal that the players were
ready; and at the third the play would begin.

During the play most of the audience listened
closely. Nowadays we go as much to *see* a play as
to hear it, but in Shakespeare's time it was the
*hearing* that was the thing. Not, as I shall show
later, that there was nothing to see; indeed there
was much; but the Elizabethans, who were not
so used to learning through their eyes, by reading
and seeing pictures, as we are to-day, were above
all things a people who liked to stay and listen.
They liked hearing music and poetry, they liked

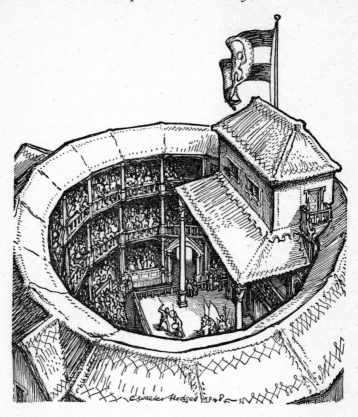

listening to witty talk: they would stand for an hour or more listening to a good sermon, and for as long as you liked at a good play. This afternoon they listened with enthusiasm to *The Spanish Tragedy*. They applauded the good actors and "mewed" (so we are told) at the bad ones, but otherwise were rather more quiet than usual. The only disturbance was when the cutpurse was caught red-handed. He was taken and tied up to one of the posts on the stage, and in the intervals between the acts he was used as an aiming mark for apple-cores.

The play at last drew to a close; the trumpets sounded a slow march; the "bodies" were carried off; the haggard ghost of Revenge promised to pursue the villains of the piece down—

> "to deepest hell
> Where none but Furies, bugs, and tortures dwell"—

and thereupon disappeared through a trap-door in the floor of the stage. The audience roared approval and then settled down for the last part of the show; for these afternoons were always rounded off with a sort of farcical performance known as a "jig", which was a piece for the clowns and Merry Andrews, made up of puns and back-chat, topical burlesque and lively dancing. The better class of patrons did not stay for it, and along with these Master Henslowe's two quiet men slipped out and went home to copy out their notes.

When all was over, and as the doors were being closed on the last of the departing audience, it started to rain again. Old Burbage, pleased with himself for having been so lucky, retired to his counting-house to reckon up the takings. The total had to be shared out, about half of it going to his partner, who owned what was called the "housekeeping" share of the business, and who kept the building in repair and paid the gatherers and other house servants; and the remainder coming to himself, for him to share again with his actors and stage-keepers, to buy stage equipment and pay the author. By the time he and his partner had worked it all out, the evening was growing dark. Most of the players had gone; the stage-keepers had tidied away to-day's gear and had got out the new stuff for the morrow. Master Shakespeare brought him the key of the chest where the playbooks were safely locked away, and went off to supper in London with Thomas Kyd and his friends. Richard had gone on ahead with some of the musicians. Old Burbage, who had had enough of boisterous evenings in his younger days, now preferred to sup at home with his wife. On his way out of the Theatre he looked up and saw that they had left the flag still flying in the rain. He called out to have it hauled down, and when he had seen it done made his way home alone through the gathering dark.

Presently the caretaker, who had been at supper in the ale-house, came in and locked the door. He

retired, yawning, behind the curtains at the back
of the stage, and lit a candle to make his bed.
When that was done he blew the candle out, and
was soon asleep. In Queen Elizabeth's time they
went to bed early and saved candles.


## 6. *The Upstart Crow*

When Shakespeare first arrived in London the
art of writing plays was, as we have seen, still
new, and it was to be left for Shakespeare himself
to show the world what could be done with it.
Still, there were already a number of clever
experimental writers from whom he learned
much of his craft. Plays in those days were often
written by two or three authors working together,
and it is often not possible to tell who wrote which
section of any particular play. For instance,
included among Shakespeare's earliest works are
the three parts of the historical play *Henry VI*.
It is not known how much of this he actually
wrote himself, but it is believed that parts of it
are in fact the work of other men. Thomas Kyd
may have had a hand in it, and so may George
Peele and Robert Greene, both famous poets in
their time.

George Peele was known more for his colourful

39

bohemian life than for his plays. We hear of him at one time as the friend of wealthy City merchants, and as the creator of pageants for the Lord Mayor's Show; at another, as a penniless actor unable to pay his rent, and unable to leave the house (because his landlady had pawned all his clothes) until in a corner of the cellar he found an old rusty suit of armour, in which he made his escape, to the great amusement of the people in the street. Then we hear of him in an escapade near Oxford where he was travelling with a troupe of players. Fascinated by a pretty girl whose father was supposed to be an invalid, he contrived to get into their house disguised as a doctor. Just for the fun of the thing, he mixed up for the old man a horrible brew concocted of all the vilest things he could lay his hands on at random, and having got his "patient" to swallow it, he went away, with the expectation of never seeing him again. But on his way home some days later he was discovered and reluctantly obliged to go back to the house, to view, as he thought, the corpse of his victim. But far from it: the old man was not only alive and kicking: he had never been so well for years; and wanted only to reward the "learned doctor" with a sumptuous dinner, in return for his miraculous cure!

These stories, with others of the kind, appeared

in a book called *The Merrie Jests of George Peele*, which was published a few years after his death. They are most unlikely to be true; they are more like the plots of "jigs" and farces than incidents in real life, but they do show the sort of reputation Peele left behind him. Perhaps, therefore, it is surprising to know that he also left a number of plays containing some poetry of quite unusual charm.

A more considerable man was Robert Greene. He was one of the typical poor scholars of that age, who having worked his way through the University found himself still poor in a world which offered him nothing but the chance to live by his wits. So he lived a dissolute life, half in, half out of the gutter, with a bully named Cutting Ball, a street gangster, for his companion. He earned his living by writing plays, books, pamphlets, novels, anything he could sell, and indeed became one of the most popular authors of the time; but of all his work his fame now rests chiefly on a few sentences he wrote shortly before he died. They are about William Shakespeare, and are the first mention of him since he came to London. Strangely enough, Greene has not a friendly word to say for him! Instead he calls him an "upstart crow", describes him as having a "tiger's heart wrapped in a player's

hide", and warns his fellow-writers to beware
of him as one who would steal their work and
their credit for his own. "He supposes," wrote
Greene, "that he is as well able to bombast out
a blank verse with the best of you; and being
an absolute *Johannes factotum*, is in his own conceit
the only *Shake-scene* in a country." This attack
was published in 1592 in a pamphlet sometimes
called *Greene's Repentance*, which he wrote in the
last stages of poverty and disease, dying all alone
in a slum room over a cobbler's shop. It was the
sneer of a jealous and disappointed man who saw
how Shakespeare's reputation was rising where
his own had fallen away. There is a story that
soon after, when Greene lay dead, the cobbler's
wife crept up to his room and put a wreath of
bay on his head. She was the only person who remembered what a famous poet he once had been.

But most famous of all the poet-dramatists
before Shakespeare, was Christopher Marlowe.
Better than anyone before, he found a way to
choose and combine words so that they had an
effect of enchantment in which he carried his
audience away in their imaginations to share
the life of a kind of tapestry-world which he
created for them on the stage, full of extreme and
violent romance. His greatest plays, *Tamburlaine*,
*Doctor Faustus*, and the *History of Edward II*,

are among the finest things in English. Had Marlowe lived longer he might have rivalled Shakespeare himself; but his life, like Greene's, was spent in unsettled times and in queer company. While he was the friend of Sir Walter Raleigh and his circle on the one hand, he mixed with spies and jailbirds on the other. When he was only twenty-nine he was mysteriously stabbed to death in a brawl in the back room of a tavern in Deptford. This happened in 1593, the year after Greene had died; and with it Shakespeare suddenly found himself for the time being without any rival at all.

## 7.  *Shakespeare's Progress*

The thing that had made Robert Greene so bitterly jealous, and the thing that is so difficult to explain, is that Shakespeare had talent of a kind which is beyond all common explanation, and to which we give the name "genius". Greene and his friends prided themselves on their scholarly training, their University degrees and so on. Shakespeare had none; he was not considered to be an "educated" man in the formal sense. Yet he was born with a skill the others did not have, and when he took up his pen his skill produced itself with the ease of second nature. His friends reported in admiration that "in his writing, (whatsoever he penned) he never blotted out line".

Among his earliest plays are *The Taming of the Shrew*, *Love's Labour's Lost*, and *Richard III*, and we find even by this time that Shakespeare, the player from the Theatre, was also quite at home with the cultured life of Queen Elizabeth's Court. Then, in the year Marlowe was killed, there began a dreadful outbreak of the plague in London, which lasted for nearly two years. The playhouses were closed and the players scattered. Shakespeare at this time wrote and published his two narrative poems, *Venus and Adonis* and *Lucrece*, both of which he dedicated to the young Earl of Southampton, who now became his friend and patron.

When the playhouses opened their doors again, in 1594, Shakespeare was ready with *Romeo and Juliet*, and with that play his great successes began. There followed *A Midsummer Night's Dream*, *Richard II*, *The Merchant of Venice* and the two parts of *Henry IV*, at which it is said Queen Elizabeth laughed so much at the character of the fat Sir John Falstaff that she asked Shakespeare to write another play showing Sir John in love; and it was to fulfil this personal request of the

Queen's that Shakespeare wrote *The Merry Wives of Windsor*.

Shakespeare's success was due not only to his genius, but to the good fortune of his entering the stage world at a time when, as we have seen, it was rapidly growing in influence and popularity, as no form of entertainment had ever done before. Besides this (and in spite of Greene's bitter remarks), Shakespeare was a very popular, likeable man. He also appears to have been a good business man, for before many years were out he had become one of the principal partners, together with Richard Burbage, in the company which owned and managed the Theatre. He began to grow rich.

## 8. *Top of the Bill*

It is now time to say something of the famous actors of that day, especially of Richard Burbage, star of his father's company at the Theatre; and of Edward Alleyn, star of the rival company at the Rose.

We first hear of Richard Burbage in the course of a lawsuit (one of many) involving the management of the Theatre. Some men had come there with a court order to collect a debt. Old James

Burbage had shut the door in their faces, and he and his wife were both leaning out of an upper window, shouting abuses at them and bidding them clear off; when in the middle of it all

Richard appeared on the scene and set about the wretched men with a broomstick. According to one witness, who tried to intervene on their behalf, "the said Richard Burbage, scornfully and disdainfully playing with this witness's nose, said he would beat him also, and did challenge the field of him at that time". This appears to have been a typical Burbage family scene. There was a shindy rather like it which, as we shall see, contributed to the building of the Globe. Richard Burbage became a particular friend of Shakespeare's, and is thought to have been the creator of many, if not all, of his great tragic heroes—Hamlet, King Lear, Macbeth and Othello. He was particularly famous for his performance of Richard III.

In the picture opposite I show him wearing the Elizabethan version of a "Roman" costume in the name part of Shakespeare's *Titus Andronicus*. The dress is interesting because it is derived from a drawing, the only one of its kind believed to be in existence, made by someone who actually saw the play on an Elizabethan stage.

Richard Burbage died in 1619, and ended his famous life with a famously appropriate epitaph. It was simply: "Exit Burbage."

His great rival, Edward Alleyn, was especially noted for his performance in the plays of

Christopher Marlowe: as Tamburlaine, Doctor Faustus and Barabbas, the Jew of Malta. The picture opposite shows him in the part of Tamburlaine, and the particular incident is in the second part of the play, at Act IV, Scene III, which opens as follows:—

*Enter* TAMBURLAINE, *drawn in his chariot by the* KINGS OF TREBIZON AND SORIA, *with bits in their mouths, reins in his left hand, and in his right hand a whip with which he scourgeth them.* . . .

TAMB.   *Holla, ye pamper'd jades of Asia,*
      *What, can ye draw but twenty miles a day,*
      *And have so proud a chariot at your heels*
      *And such a coachman as great Tamburlaine.* . .

The dress he wears is the Elizabethan version of an "oriental" costume.

Being of Henslowe's Company, Alleyn did not have the chance to work with Shakespeare, and much he may have regretted it. If so, it can have been his only regret. Hand in glove with Henslowe, whose stepdaughter Joan he married, he came to inherit Henslowe's prosperous business, and retired early from the stage, a wealthy man. He then founded the College of God's Gift at Dulwich, whose boys ever since have called themselves "Alleynians". Together with his college he left for posterity a collection of papers,

49

diaries and account-books once belonging to Henslowe and himself, which are now the most valuable record we have of the stage life of his time. Among them are some letters he wrote to his wife while he was away in the country with his company, then called Lord Strange's Men. They give so vivid a picture of his life that it does not come amiss to quote one here in full. It was written from Bristol in 1593, the year of a terrible plague in London:

My Good Sweet Mouse,

I commend me heartily to you and to my father, my mother, and my sister Bess, hoping in God though the sickness be round about you yet, by His mercy, it may escape your house, which, by the grace of God, it shall. Therefore use this course: keep your house fair and clean, which I know you will, and every evening throw water before your door, and in your back side, and have in your windows good store of rue and herb of grace, and with all the grace of God, which must be obtained by prayers; and so doing, no doubt but the Lord will mercifully defend you.

Now, good mouse, I have no news to send you but this, that we have all our health, for which the Lord be praised. I received your letter at Bristow, by Richard Cowley, for which I thank you.

I have sent you by this bearer, Thomas Pope's kins-man, my white waistcoat, because it is a trouble to me to carry it. Receive it with this letter, and lay it up for me till I come.

If you send any more letters, send to me by the carriers of Shrewsbury or to West Chester or to York, to be kept till my Lord Strange's players come.

And thus, sweetheart, with my hearty commendations to all our friends, I cease from Bristow this Wednesday after St. James his day, being ready to begin the play of *Harry of Cornwall*.

Mouse, do my hearty commends to Mr Grigs' wife and all his household, and to my sister Philips.

Your loving husband,

E. ALLEYN.

The two greatest comic actors of the period were Richard Tarlton and Will Kempe. Tarlton, it is true, was a little before Shakespeare's day (he died in 1588) but he was so well remembered throughout Shakespeare's lifetime that he has a right to be mentioned here. He is said to have been the original of the jester Yorick, whom Hamlet speaks of in the play. He was the Queen's favourite clown. A memory of him, published in later years, is that "when Queen Elizabeth was *serious* (I dare not say *sullen*) and out of *good humour*, he could *un-dumpish* her at his pleasure". He was at one time the leader of a company called "The Queen's Men", for whom he wrote plays and jigs, and there is a story of them in the country, and of a pompous local Justice who came to see their show: "They were now entering into their first merriment (as they call it), and the people began exceedingly to laugh when Tarlton first peeped out his head. Whereat the Justice, not a little moved, and seeing with his becks and nods he could not make them cease, he went with his staff and beat them on the bare pates, in that they, being but farmers and poor country hinds, would presume to laugh at the Queen's men, and make no more account of her cloth in his presence."

Tarlton's portrait on page 51, which I have adapted from a woodcut on the cover of a book called *Tarlton's Jests* (*Full of Delight, Wit, and*

Will Kempe

*Honest Mirth*), shows him stepping a dance to
the accompaniment of his own pipe and tabor.
Clowning and dancing went together. This was
especially so in the case of the famous clown Will
Kempe. As a dancer he held (and probably still
holds) the world's long-distance record, for in
1597 he laid a wager he would dance a morris
from London to Norwich: which he did. It took
him nine days, and his going was something like
a triumph. All the way along when they heard he

was coming, people flocked to see him pass, and when he reached Norwich he had hardly room to dance through the crowd. He was welcomed by the Mayor and Guilds of the City, who gave him a life pension, made him a freeman of their city, and nailed up his dancing shoes in the Guildhall in memory of the great occasion. He afterwards wrote the full story of the exploit in a little book, *Kempe's Nine Days Wonder*, from the cover of which I have taken his portrait. It shows him with his piper, Thomas Sly.

On the stage he acted with the Burbage company. He is known to have played in Shakespeare's *Romeo and Juliet* and *Much Ado About Nothing*, in which he created the part of Constable Dogberry. He must also have been one of the clowns in *A Midsummer Night's Dream*: did he perhaps play Bottom the Weaver?

## 9.  *The Boy Players*

It is well known that women never appeared on the stage in Shakespeare's day, and women's parts were always played by boys. They were apprenticed when they were about ten years old to individual actors, who were responsible for training them and paying them their wages; and they remained apprentices until they were fifteen or sixteen. They were required to have good voices, a talent for acting, and if possible some talent for music as well. They had frequently to sing and play the lute. It will be noted that there are usually not many women's parts in the action of an Elizabethan play, but the few there are often demand a high degree of skill. Juliet and Lady Macbeth, for example, are not parts for actors of poor quality, and Shakespeare, writing for players whose individual abilities he knew well, would never have written such parts had he not been sure that they would be rendered in a way to do them justice.

It is interesting to recall, by the way, the use Shakespeare makes of the device of dressing up his heroines in boys' clothes, as for example in *Twelfth Night* and *As You Like It*: a simple but clever way of turning the condition to advantage.

But as well as the boy apprentices in the men's companies there were for a time two famous companies composed entirely of boys. These were "The Children of Paul's" and "The Children of the Chapel Royal". Originally they had been recruited solely as choirboys, but being under Royal patronage they were sometimes used to give recitals at Court entertainments, and having well-trained voices and a pretty way of speaking verse, their choirmasters put them to learning and reciting plays. It may be imagined that the boys entered into the spirit of the thing with a will, and their performances soon became so fashionable that for a while they became serious rivals to the men's companies in the public playhouses. The children did not play in public, but in so-called "private" playhouses, where the conditions were very different. They had covered halls, they performed in the evening by candlelight, and they admitted only the better sort of audience, not the groundling riff-raff of the open houses. Their theatres were in the City itself, the Children of the Chapel Royal at Blackfriars, the Children of Paul's, as their name implies, in a building by the Cathedral.

Of course we must suppose that these boys were mostly willing members of their companies, but their acting abilities were for a time so profitable to their masters that those gentlemen began to make very free use of the special authority they had to enlist boys as "choristers" in the Royal Chapels. In one case they actually kidnapped a boy on his way home from school, and his father had to take the matter to the Privy Council before he could get him released. And a famous actor of later years, one Nathan Field, was said to have been started on his career, when a boy, in just such a way as this.

The plays written for the boys' companies were no different from those of any other company. There was not the slightest attempt to make them "fit for children". On the contrary, there was a time when they specialised in the most horrific kinds of blood-and-thunder plays which, from their being acted almost in darkness, save for the light of one or two eerie candles, came to be known as "nocturnals".

Of their comedies, *The Knight of the Burning Pestle*, by Beaumont and Fletcher, is still a favourite, but it is not always realised that this play was written to be acted entirely by children.

## 10. *The End of the "Theatre"*

You will remember that old James Burbage had built the Theatre on a plot of ground for which he had a lease of only twenty-one years. In the twenty-first year he died, leaving the Theatre to his two sons, Richard and Cuthbert. Since their tenancy of the ground on which it was built was then on the point of running out, this bequest was of doubtful value. The brothers sent to the landlord, asking him to renew the lease.

The landlord did not reply. It must be admitted that the Burbage family were not the best of tenants; their twenty-one years had been notable for brawls and riots. The landlord would have been glad to be rid of them; and besides, he reckoned the Burbages, when their lease expired, would have to leave the Theatre, with the ground it stood on, to him. There was a fortune in it. So when they sent to him he simply did not answer.

To this the Burbage brothers, with Shakespeare and their other partners, guessing what was in the wind, had a ready answer. They rented another plot of ground over on Bankside; they engaged a builder—Peter Street, his name was—who just after Christmas in the year 1598 began to pull down the Theatre and to cart its timbers over the river for rebuilding on the new site.

As soon as he heard of this, the landlord tried hard to have it stopped. He claimed that Street, the builder, was trespassing on his ground, and sent some men to prevent him carting the stuff away; whereupon, as he complained to the magistrates afterwards, the Burbage party "then and there armed themselves with diverse and many unlawful and offensive weapons, as namely swords, daggers, bills, axes and such like, and so armed did then repair unto the said Theatre, and then and there armed as aforesaid, in very

riotous, outrageous and forcible manner . . .
attempted to pull down the said Theatre". His
own people, he said, were "going about in
peaceable manner to procure them to desist from
that unlawful enterprise". But in vain: the
Burbage party resisted strongly, "pulling, break-
ing and throwing down the said Theatre in very
outrageous, violent and riotous sort".

At least they did not throw it down so violently
that it could not be rebuilt. From the timbers of
the old Theatre a fine new playhouse was created,
which hoisted its flag for the first time in the
autumn nine months later. This was the Globe,
most famous of all the playhouses, and the birth-
place of most of Shakespeare's greatest plays.

## 11.  *The "Globe"*

We nowadays are so used to the methods of
our modern stages, with their splendid effects of
artificial scenery and lighting, prepared in secret
and revealed as if by magic from behind curtains,
that we find it hard to believe a play put on
without these special things could be equally
exciting. Yet when Shakespeare put on his own
plays at the Globe, they were just as effective
then under the open sky as they are to-day

behind footlights; it is only that the effects he used were different. A favourite one, for example, which used to thrill Elizabethan audiences to the marrow, and which for obvious reasons we never use to-day, was the shooting off of cannon: remember that in *Henry V*, at the end of King Henry's famous rally before the walls of Harfleur, the stirring final cry of "God for Harry, England, and Saint George!" was the signal for a magnificent cannonade outside, and the actual smell of gunpowder would have hung in the air during all the rest of the battle. Then there is the familiar stage direction "Enter with drums and colours..." We may have the colours nowadays, but we get very little of the excitement the Elizabethans expected from their drums; neither for that matter do we have our trumpets blowing fanfares full on the stage as they did. Ours are smuggled away behind—"trumpets small within", as Shakespeare put it, in one of his stage directions; but that was for a special effect of distance, and usually his audience had their trumpets big. And besides this, although at the Globe there was not much in the way of painted scenery as we understand it to-day, there was a great deal of ornament and decoration. Visitors were much impressed by the wooden columns "which, painted like marble, could deceive the most expert". We must imagine the stage, painted as gay as a fair or a circus, hung with garlands and coloured tapestries and with banners stirring in the wind. Shakespeare's audience loved bright colours and rich dresses, spectacular scenes with kings on high thrones, devils springing out of trap-doors with a fizz and bang of fireworks, and gods and goddesses descending on clouds from Heaven: they loved processions, drums, flags and fighting, and when there was a battle going on in the Globe the trumpets and shouting could be heard right across the river.

What, then, was the Globe playhouse really like, in detail, and how were Shakespeare's plays put on? And here it must be sadly confessed that we do not exactly know. The builder's plans have all been lost, and although we have other sources of information upon which to base a fairly accurate reconstruction, there is some difference of opinion about details. The drawing I give on pages 62 and 63 is as reliable as any, and with its help let us, in imagination, go in and study the place.

There seems to be nobody about except for an old man sweeping up apple-cores in the yard. We will go in round the back.

All this part of the building behind the stage is known as the "tiring-house", that is, the place where the actors attire themselves for the play.

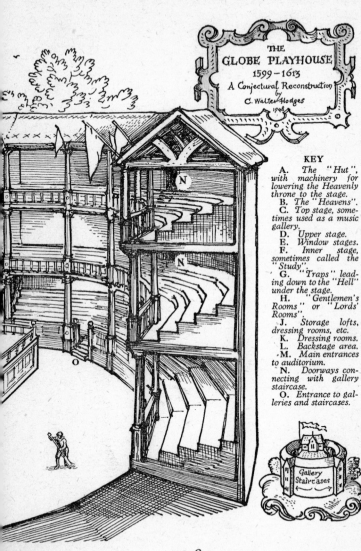

THE
GLOBE PLAYHOUSE
1599-1613
A Conjectural Reconstruction
by
C. Walter Hodges
1948

## KEY

**A.** The "Hut", with machinery for lowering the Heavenly throne to the stage.

**B.** The "Heavens".

**C.** Top stage, sometimes used as a music gallery.

**D.** Upper stage.

**E.** Window stages.

**F.** Inner stage, sometimes called the "Study".

**G.** "Traps" leading down to the "Hell" under the stage.

**H.** "Gentlemen's Rooms" or "Lords' Rooms".

**J.** Storage lofts, dressing rooms, etc.

**K.** Dressing rooms.

**L.** Backstage area.

**M.** Main entrances to auditorium.

**N.** Doorways connecting with gallery staircase.

**O.** Entrance to galleries and staircases.

Gallery Staircases

63

On the ground-level we find tables and benches, a looking-glass, and all sorts of properties set out ready for this afternoon's performance. It is what to-day we would call the "green-room"; and here is the prompter's place (they called him the "bookholder"), with his copy of the play lying ready on a stool. And looking around us what a crowd of stuff we find stored here in every corner! There is a wonderful collection of dresses. The Elizabethan stage was renowned for the splendour and extravagance of its attire. Here stuffed in baskets, there hanging along the wall, are the fantastic accoutrements of Roman and Turkish guise, pageant armour crested and painted, apparel for gods and goddesses, ghosts and devils, nymphs, heroes and fairies, a "cloak for to go invisible" and "a doublet of white satin laid thick with gold lace"—this last being but one of a multitude of rich courtly clothes which the players used to buy at second-hand from the wardrobes of noblemen and dandies, those "feathered estriches" who wore their fortunes on their backs. Besides all this, here, too, are stage "properties" of every imaginable kind. Thrones, tombs, caves, a "Hell Mouth":

*Item*, 1 wooden canopy; old Mahomet's head.
*Item*, 1 lion skin; 1 bear's skin; and Phaeton's limbs and Phaeton's chariot; and Argus's head.

64

*Item*, Neptune's fork and garland.
*Item*, 1 crosier staff; Kent's wooden leg.
*Item*, Iris's head, and rainbow; 1 little altar.

The above is quoted from a list of Henslowe's effects as given in his own diary; but it will do equally well for the property-room of the Globe. The list goes on and on, quoting at random a tree of golden apples, Mercury's wings, two coffins, a dragon, a "Cloth of the Sun and Moon" and a hundred and one other things, including "a frame for the heading", which was a piece of trick machinery to give the illusion of someone being beheaded.

Much of this is stored in the space underneath the stage, where, bending our heads a little, we now make our way along. This, following the old custom of the medieval Mystery Plays, is known as the "Hell", and here are two trap-doors, through which ghosts and devils can be made to rise up on to the stage. We open one, knocking away the post that supports it from beneath, and climb through. The stage, where we now find ourselves, is large and high, and is surrounded by a railing. At the back leading into the tiring-house are two doors and, between them, a large recess which can be closed with a pair of curtains. This is in constant use during performances, for here are staged the occasional "set pieces" which require preparation while the play is going on out in front: the king's throne, or the table for a banquet, can be set here and "discovered" by the drawing aside of the curtains when ready. Above this recess we see a gallery, flanked by two openings called windows. This gallery is one of the most typical and useful features of the Elizabethan stage, and serves variously for an upper room, as in the beginning of *The Taming of the Shrew*, or the poop of a ship or, most common of all, the battlements of a castle or town; and as for the windows, it is at one of these that Juliet appears while Romeo watches her from the "orchard" below. Now looking higher still, we see one other gallery. It is covered by a blue curtain patterned with stars to represent the sky, and it is usually supposed to be a part of "the Heavens", the name given to all the upper part of the stage, and particularly to the stage roof, the under side of which is richly decorated with paintings of the sun, moon and stars, and the signs of the Zodiac. Gods and goddesses are sometimes presented throned in glory in this high gallery: but to-day, when we climb up there by a ladder in the tiring-house, we find only some benches with sheets of music and instruments all ready, for the place is often used as a music gallery. Coming from here, unseen behind the starry curtain, the music can be made to have an effect of magic, of being in the air; for example, when, in *The Tempest*, Prospero magically summons his "heavenly music", it is from up here in the Heavens that it sounds.

There is one more ladder, leading to the highest part of all, the hut over the top of the stage. In here we find the winding gear which lets down the flying chariot in which the gods descend to earth. As has been said before, this was a popular feature of many Elizabethan shows, but the descent had its mechanical difficulties: the machine creaked, and the noise had to be disguised by the "airy music", or better still by peals of thunder, most effectively produced by rolling cannon balls up and down on the wooden floor of the hut.

There is a door at the side of the hut, leading out to the little balcony from which they hoist the flag, and as we stand out here, looking over the thatched roof, we see to our surprise that an audience is assembling in the playhouse below. The players, we find, have suddenly returned, the musicians are tuning up their instruments, and one of them, trumpet in hand, is coming up here to blow the first sounding from our balcony. Let us go down quickly and find a good place to watch the play.

## 12. *A Performance of* Richard III

The play to be performed is Shakespeare's
*Richard III*, in which Richard Burbage made
such a great success when it was first performed
eight years since. He is to appear again this
afternoon in the title rôle, and, although it is an
old play, big crowds have come to see him. The
place is full everywhere, from the Lords' Rooms
to the yard, and we were lucky to find a seat
where our view of the back of the stage is not
obscured by either of the two big pillars support-
ing the Heavens. Now, at the second sounding,
a number of dandies come out from the tiring-
house with stools in their hands, and seat themselves out of the way at the sides of the stage. It
is rather a hot afternoon, and already it is
getting a bit stuffy—even a bit smelly—in here:
perhaps when the play starts . . . but there
goes the third sounding, and there—enormous
applause!—Burbage, as Richard of Gloucester,
steps through the curtains on to the stage to begin
the play.

On the following pages are sketches of some of
the scenes from *Richard III* as they might have
appeared that afternoon at the Globe.

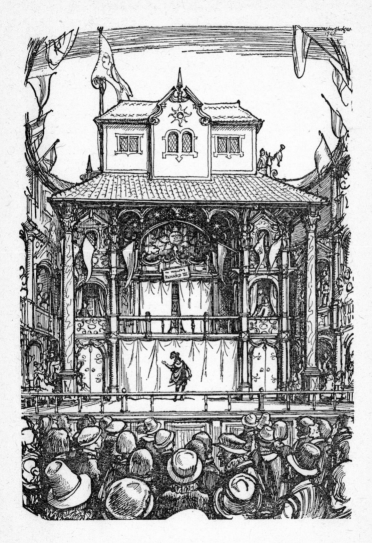

## *Richard III: Act I, Scene ii*

*Enter the corpse of King Henry the Sixth, Gentlemen with halberds
to guard it; Lady Anne being the mourner.*

ANNE.  *Set down, set down your honourable load—
If honour may be shrouded in a hearse—
Whilst I awhile obsequiously lament
The untimely fall of virtuous Lancaster.
Poor key-cold figure of a holy king!
Pale ashes of the house of Lancaster! . . .*

Thus the scene is set, not with painted scenery,
but with the royal hearse, the halberds, the slow
march, and possibly also the slow beat of a drum
and the tolling of a bell.  The Lady Anne (the
part is, of course, played here by a boy) is the
widow of King Henry's son Edward, murdered
by the crookbacked Richard of Gloucester, who
soon enters the stage.  The picture shows the
moment where he admits that he is the murderer
of the old King Henry also, and offers to let her
kill him:

*[He lays his breast open: she offers at it with his sword.*

*Nay, do not pause, for I did kill King Henry,
But 'twas thy beauty that provoked me.
Nay, now dispatch; 'twas I that stabbed young Edward,
But 'twas thy heavenly face that set me on.*

*[Here she lets fall the sword.*

## *Richard III: Act I, Scene iv*

The stage now represents a place in the Tower of London, where the Duke of Clarence is a prisoner. While he sleeps, there enter the two murderers sent by his brother Richard.

SECOND MURDERER. *Come, shall we to this gear?*

FIRST MURDERER. *Take him over the costard with the hilts of thy sword, and then we will chop him in the malmsey-butt in the next room.*

SECOND MURDERER. *O excellent device! Make a sop of him!*

FIRST MURDERER. *Hark, he stirs: shall I strike?*

SECOND MURDERER. *No, first let's reason with him.*

(Fatal weakness for a professional murderer! The Duke reasons too well, and the Second Murderer's conscience begins to stir. In the end it is the First Murderer alone who takes the Duke over the costard.)

FIRST MURDERER. *Take that and that: if all this will not do,*
*I'll drown you in the malmsey-butt within.*

[*Exit, with the body.*

### *Richard III: Act III, Scene v*

*Enter* BUCKINGHAM, DERBY, HASTINGS, THE BISHOP OF ELY, RATCLIFFE, LOVEL, *with others, and take their seats at a table.*

Lord Hastings, who has refused to take part in Richard's machinations to make himself king, is in the toils. Richard comes to the Council to denounce him on a trumped-up charge of witch-craft, and has him hustled off to immediate death:

> *Off with his head!   Now, by Saint Paul I swear*
> *I will not dine till I have seen the same.*

This picture shows one of the ways in which the curtained part at the back of the stage was used. The table, which has to be a long one to seat all these people, has been set ready on the inner stage during the preceding scene, and is now revealed by opening the curtains. It has also been carried forward a few paces (by two or three of the less important actors) so as to be better in view of all parts of the auditorium. When the scene is over, the table will be quickly withdrawn and the curtains closed again.

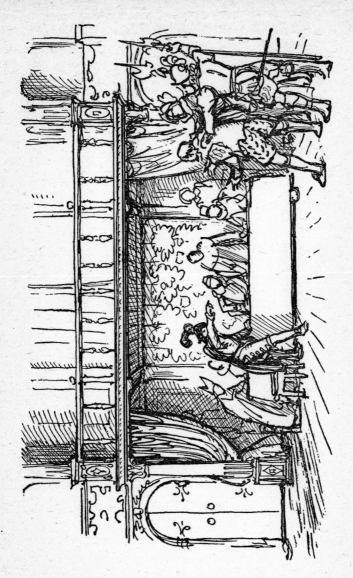

## *Richard III: Act III, Scene vii*

Richard's plot is on the point of success, and he is now ready to make himself king; but it is none the less necessary for him to seem unwilling to take the throne except at the earnest entreaty of the common people. The Duke of Buckingham, having contrived to work some of the common people into the right frame of mind, brings them with the Lord Mayor to Baynard's Castle, where Richard is waiting. Then:

> *Enter* RICHARD *aloft, between two Bishops.*
>
> MAYOR. *See where he stands between two clergymen!*
> BUCKINGHAM. *Two props of virtue for a Christian prince* . . .

"Alas," protests Richard, when the crown is offered:

> " *Why would you heap these cares on me?*
> *I am unfit for State and majesty.*"

In the foreground Catesby, Richard's follower, smiles behind his hand.

The sketch shows a common use of the upper stage, which here represents the walls of Baynard's Castle. It is quite likely, although I have not shown it, that some form of painted scenery representing battlements may sometimes have been used on these occasions, instead of the railing.

The figures which can be seen at the windows at either side of the upper stage are part of the audience. There is a big crowd and all the auditorium is full, so the stage windows have been let out as additional "boxes".

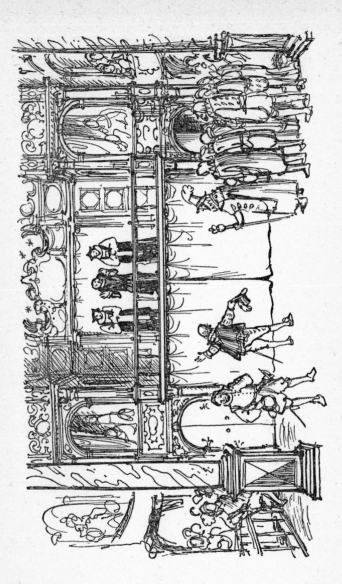

### *Richard III: Act IV, Scene ii*

The costumes being worn in this play are more or less those of Shakespeare's own time. This may make it difficult in the sketch opposite to sort out the players from the audience. Those standing in the background are players, members of Richard's court who have withdrawn to allow him to talk privately with Buckingham. Those seated are audience.

So Richard has become king, though he still does not feel secure enough on his ill-gotten throne:

*Ha! am I King? 'tis so: but Edward lives.*

He means to take the life of the young prince Edward and his brother, and intends that Buckingham shall help him. But Buckingham recoils from such a crime—and later pays with his own head for his scruples.

Notice the throne. This, sometimes called a "State", is a very hard-worked piece of Elizabethan stage furniture. Richard's throne to-day will be used by Tamburlaine or Julius Cæsar to-morrow. Perhaps a playhouse would possess two or three different thrones, but regular patrons would soon know all the customary stage properties by heart, and would be sure to notice whenever a new piece was added or an old one came out in a new coat of paint and freshly gilded, for some special play.

## *Richard III: Act V, Scene ii*

*Enter* RICHMOND, OXFORD, BLUNT, HERBERT *and others, with drum and colours.*

There is in another of Shakespeare's plays a stage direction which reads: "Drum and colours: Enter . . . the whole army." Perhaps the stage army which mustered more than some nine or ten souls, except on very special occasions, would have been lucky. In *Henry V* Shakespeare begs pardon of the audience for the small forces he is about to deploy on so splendid and legendary a battle as Agincourt:

> *And so our scene must to the battle fly;*
> *Where—O for pity!—we shall much disgrace*
> *With four or five most vile and ragged foils*
> *Right ill-disposed in brawl ridiculous*
> *The name of Agincourt.*

But surely this was an apology in form only. The entry of the stage army, with its drum and colours and flourish of trumpets, must have been as much looked forward to on an Elizabethan stage as is Cinderella's coach in a Christmas pantomime to-day, and as much applauded when at last it came marching on.

In this play the sound of Richmond's drum is the sound of retribution overtaking King Richard in the end, marching to Bosworth Field.

## *Richard III: Act V, Scene ii*

*Enter* KING RICHARD *in arms, with* NORFOLK, THE EARL OF SURREY, *and others.*

RICHARD. *Here pitch our tents, even here in Bosworth Field . . .*

So Richard's tent is put up on one side of the stage, and a little while later:

*Enter, on the other side of the field,* RICHMOND, SIR WILLIAM BRANDON, OXFORD, *and others. Some of the soldiers pitch Richmond's tent.*

The two tents, one on each side, with their flags disposed about them, represent the opposing armies. The stage between is Bosworth Field. Each in his own tent, the two leaders make their plans for the morrow and then lie down to rest.

The ghosts of Richard's eleven victims now come forth to haunt him in his sleep. "Despair and die!" they cry to him, while to Richmond they promise quiet sleep and happy victory.

> *God and good angels fight on Richmond's side;*
> *And Richard falls in height of all his pride.*

> [*The ghosts vanish.* RICHARD *starts out of his dream.*

How this was actually done we can only guess. In the picture the ghosts are shown draped in their blood-stained shrouds. Each, after he has spoken, steps back a few paces into the inner stage, which stands open all hung around with black. Then, as Richard starts up awake, the curtains are quickly closed over the inner stage, and the ghosts are no more seen.

## *Richard III: Act V, Scene v*

*Alarum. Enter* RICHARD *and* RICHMOND; *they fight.* RICHARD *is slain. Retreat and flourish. Re-enter* RICHMOND, DERBY *bearing the crown, with divers other Lords.*

RICHMOND. *God and your arms be praised, victorious friends!*
*The day is ours; the bloody dog is dead.*

DERBY. *Courageous Richmond, well hast thou acquit thee.*
*Lo, here, this long usurped royalty*
*From the dead temples of this bloody wretch*
*Have I pluck'd off, to grace thy brows withal:*
*Wear it, enjoy it, and make much of it.*

RICHMOND. *Great God of heaven, say amen to all!*

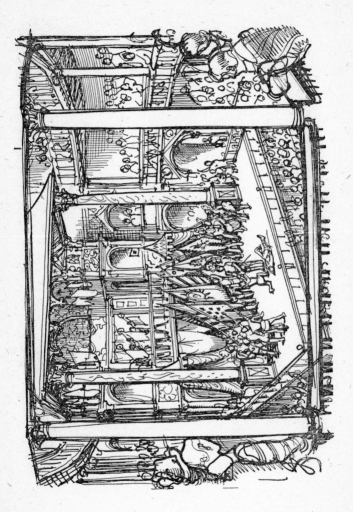

### 13. *Stage Music*

Music was employed frequently throughout all Elizabethan plays. The English were then the most musical people in the world. No playhouse was complete without its musicians — neither, for that matter, was any tavern in the town; and even barbers in their shops commonly provided a cittern or a lute for their customers to play upon while waiting to be shaved. These were stringed instruments, something like the modern guitar: though the lute had a greater range than the cittern, and was more difficult to play. Besides these, the usual stringed instruments were the treble, tenor and bass viols, and the viol-de-gamba, all played with a bow. These were something like our modern violins and 'cello; but their note was more soft, reedy and plaintive; their use on the stage gave an air of quiet sadness, such as we find at the beginning of *Twelfth Night*. The gay instruments were the wind instruments, the pipes and hautboys (oboes) of various kinds. Then there were the horns (used for hunting-music), the solemn sackbut or trombone, the drums, and of course the many trumpets for sounding flourishes, alarums, retreats, "tuckets" and other royal and military effects.

Lute

Shawms & Hautboys

Cittern

Sackbut

Viols

Viol-de-Gamba

Recorders

87

There were small bands (or "Noises") of musicians in London, who could be hired by the playhouses as occasion required ("Sneak's Noise" was a well-known one, and was mentioned by Shakespeare in *Henry IV*). But it may be that the drummers and trumpeters were part of the ordinary playhouse staff, as were the singers and lute-players, who were often found from among the boy-actors.

## 14. *Essex's Rebellion*

The Globe first opened its doors in the autumn of 1599, and one of the new plays presented there that season was Shakespeare's *Julius Cæsar*. Earlier that summer, at the Curtain, next door to the now vacant site of the old Theatre, there had been a first performance of his *Henry V*, and in the course of that play he had introduced a compliment to the great Earl of Essex who was then in Ireland waging (as Shakespeare did not know) a most feeble and unsuccessful war. Shakespeare looked forward to the Earl's victorious return, "bringing rebellion broached on his sword", and ventured to compare it with Henry V's triumphant return after Agincourt. Alas, it came out very differently. There was

more applause for the opening of the new playhouse that September than for the homecoming
of the Earl. He brought nothing with him but
an almost treacherous peace, and a following of
adventurers and malcontents whose ambitions he
had encouraged as a support for other, more
overweening, ambitions of his own. During all
the following year, perceiving that he could never
again become, as once he had been, the favourite
of the old Queen, he found himself sinking
deeper and deeper into the mire of a conspiracy,
his own, to overthrow her. By the beginning of
1601 the situation in London was critical. The
Earl, in his palace by the river, was hesitating
on the brink of open rebellion. The Queen,
knowing that he was as rash as he was popular,
cautiously bided her time and waited for him to
make a false step.

On the 6th of February, 1601, a Friday, there
came into the tiring-house of the Globe a certain
Sir Gilly Meyricke, with some of his friends, all
ardent supporters of the Earl of Essex. They
wanted to persuade the players to change whatever plans they had for the following afternoon,
and put on a performance of Shakespeare's
*Richard II* instead. The players were unwilling.
They explained that, with all the uneasiness of
the time, they were having a bad season, that

*Richard II* was an old play which was out of fashion and would not draw, and they could not risk losing money by playing it to an empty house. But Sir Gilly and his friends were very pressing. They declared they would pay in advance enough money to cover the day's takings, in addition to whatever else the players could take at the door in the ordinary way. This was a good offer, and with a little more persuasion the players accepted it. Perhaps the knight and his party stayed a little longer to explain how they wanted some certain details of the play to be brought out. Did the players suspect what was behind it all?

The point was that the story of Richard II, represented as an unworthy English sovereign turned off the throne by a popular hero, had become peculiarly linked up in people's minds with the fortunes of Essex, and in the brewing crisis Sir Gilly Meyricke's act was generally understood as an act of encouragement to the Earl's supporters and of barely concealed defiance to the Queen. Did the players understand this when they took the bribe—for that, in effect, was what it was? At least they must have had their qualms that Saturday during the performance, with Sir Gilly and all his host of friends so eagerly acclaiming every line that pointed to the deserved overthrow of a king. How relieved they must have been when the anxious afternoon passed off without incident, and their dangerous patrons had returned again over the river to the bustle of excited expectation that hung about the courtyard of Essex House.

The next morning the storm burst. The Earl marched into the City at the head of his cheering supporters to raise the citizens against the Queen. The citizens shut their doors. Soon the cheering grew less loud and the Earl's supporters remarkably less numerous. By late afternoon the citizens came out of doors again to gossip about the great fiasco; and on Bankside that evening, from the roof of the Globe, the players might have seen a little boat going up river, taking the Earl ignominiously home to Essex House. Or, next day, they might have seen the barge pass by that took him back again down river to the Tower.

The players were questioned about that suspicious Saturday performance, but nothing was held against them. They could not be blamed because a patron had paid them to act a well-known play. Evil was in the eye of the beholder.

Just a fortnight later, on the evening of the 24th of February, they were summoned to act at Court. Perhaps the Master of the Revels had been advised to provide some distraction for the

Queen, to keep her from thinking too much about the days, not very long past, when Essex had been her devoted favourite and the hero of her Court. We do not know what performance the players gave that night, and we may well wonder how much of it the aged Queen listened to as she sat there with the candle-light twinkling on her rich clothes.

Essex was beheaded next morning.


## 15. *Ben Jonson and Others*

In 1603 King James I came to the throne. Shakespeare by this time was a well-to-do man, owner of a large house in his home town of Stratford on Avon, and entitled to his own coat of arms. He was William Shakespeare, gentleman, of Stratford upon Avon; poet, playwright, player, and "Master-Sharer" of the Globe; and his company was now honoured by the new King with the title of "The King's Players". King James proved to be an enthusiastic patron of all forms of theatrical entertainment, and the players now flourished more than ever before. This was the period when Shakespeare wrote his four great tragedies, *Hamlet*, *Othello*, *King Lear* and *Macbeth* —a play with a Scottish setting, in compliment to the nationality of the new king.

But Shakespeare was now no longer without his rivals. Greatest of these was (and still is) Benjamin Jonson. He was a big, brilliant, quarrelsome man. As a youth he had been a soldier, fighting against the Spaniards in the Netherlands. In later life he escaped hanging only by a hair-breadth, after he had killed a bully in a duel; he got away with the punishment of being branded on his left thumb with the letter T — for Tyburn, the place of common execution. It was said that Shakespeare was the first to recognise his genius as a playwright. Jonson had shown his play *Every Man in his Humour* to Burbage, who had refused it; but Shakespeare, having called Jonson back, read the play himself, and persuaded Burbage to change his mind. Shakespeare himself took a part in it when it was performed. It proved to be one of the greatest of English comedies. Others that Jonson wrote are *The Alchemist* and *The Silent Woman*.

Besides Ben Jonson there were now so many well-known playwrights that there is no room here to mention more than a few by name. But let us, for a moment, join a group of them at supper at the Mermaid Tavern in Cheapside in, say, the year 1604. It is April the 23rd, Shakespeare's fortieth birthday, and his friends have invited him to a celebration. Shakespeare is

1943

at the head of the table; on his right, Richard
Burbage has risen to propose his health; on his
left sits Ben Jonson; next to Jonson is Thomas
Dekker, who wrote the play *The Shoemaker's
Holiday*. (He also wrote an interesting book about
the life and tricks of thieves and beggars in
London, from which I quoted a little earlier on.)

94

Opposite him sits Thomas Heywood, who claimed to have had a hand in the writing of more than two hundred plays. Next is John Webster, author of the *Duchess of Malfi*; next again, John Marston (who might not have come here to supper had he known Ben Jonson was here, for the two had been publicly quarrelling for years about each other's

95

plays); and at the end of the table Francis Beaumont and John Fletcher, the famous partnership of friends who lived and worked together and were joint authors, among much else, of *The Knight of the Burning Pestle*.

In the background is Master Sneak and his "Noyse".

## 16. *The Court Masques*

It was Ben Jonson who was chiefly responsible for the return to fashion of the Court Masque. This was rather like a stately pantomime or charade, arranged with poetry, dancing, music, and elaborate scenery and dresses, for the private pleasure of the King and his Court. The principal parts were often taken by members of the royal family, or by courtiers, though sometimes professional players were employed as well. It was not a new form of entertainment, but under the patronage of King James it now took on a new and splendid lease of life. Thousands of pounds would be spent for a masque for one night.

Ben Jonson proved to have a special talent for devising this kind of show, and he was fortunate in having to work with a partner as brilliant as himself. This was Inigo Jones, who was not only

a great architect, but had also, while travelling in Italy, made a special study of the new types of theatrical scenery and effects which were being developed there. Many of his designs for these Court Masques have been preserved, and the scenery shown in the picture on page 97 is based upon some of them.

It shows the masque of *Oberon, the Faery Prince*, which was produced by Jonson and Inigo Jones on New Year's Day, 1611. It was given in The Banqueting Hall at Westminster, in honour of Henry, Prince of Wales, who probably himself took the part of Oberon. This show opened in front of a "cliff", before which some "Sylvans and Satyrs" appeared. After the action had gone a little way the "cliff" parted in the middle and drew back, revealing the outside of a fairy castle. There followed an "antick dance", which ended suddenly with the crowing of a cock; and upon this the castle itself opened, showing inside a scene in fairyland, with Oberon the Faery Prince mounted in a chariot drawn by two white bears, and attended by all his Court.

The growing fashion for shows of this kind can be seen reflected in most of Shakespeare's later plays. They are plays of fantasy and romance, and were staged with more elaborate dresses and effects than Shakespeare had been accustomed to use in earlier days. In *Cymbeline* there is a scene where Jupiter descends from the Heavens on an eagle; in *Pericles* there is a pageant boat on wheels which is "sailed" in through the yard and moored alongside the stage; and in *The Tempest*, his last play, there is included a masque in which nymphs and shepherds and goddesses come forth to celebrate the betrothal of Ferdinand and Miranda.

## 17. *Shakespeare Goes Home*

On the 29th of June, 1613, there was presented at the Globe a new play about Henry VIII. It may have been Shakespeare's own play; but whether this was so or not, the performance that day was never finished. What happened is told in a letter written by a certain Sir Henry Wotton to his nephew, a few days later:

"Now, to let matters of state sleep, I will entertain you at the present with what has happened this week at the Bank's side. The King's Players had a new play called *All is True*, representing some principal pieces of the reign of Henry VIII, which was set forth with many extraordinary circumstances of pomp and majesty.

. . . Now, King Henry making a masque at the Cardinal Wolsey's house, and certain chambers * being shot off at his entry, some of the paper, or other stuff, wherewith one of them was stopped, did light on the thatch, where being thought at first but an idle smoke, and their eyes more attentive to the show, it kindled inwardly and ran round like a train, consuming within less than an hour the whole house to the very grounds. . . . Yet nothing did perish but wood and straw, and a few forsaken cloaks; only one man had his breeches set on fire, that would perhaps have broiled him, if he had not by the benefit of a provident wit put it out with bottle ale."

So ended the Globe. Or, rather, so ended the timbers of the old Theatre : for the Globe was rebuilt and open again by the following summer, by all accounts more splendid than before.

And with the burning of the first Globe we may end our short account of Shakespeare and his theatre. For some years he had been spending more and more of his time at his home in Stratford, quietly assuming the dignities of a well-to-do citizen. By the time the Globe was burned he was not often seen in London. Quite suddenly, three

* *i.e.* cannons.

years later, on his fifty-second birthday, he died. He was buried at Stratford.

But for our last picture of him let us see him at home in his garden on a summer's evening a few years before. With him are his daughter Susanna, her husband and their little girl; and his younger daughter Judith.

He has been writing, and now it is supper-time; they have come to help him to carry in his things.